CALM MONSTERS, KIND MONSTERS

A **SESAME STREET** GUIDE TO **MINDFULNESS**

Karen Latchana Kenney

Lerner Publications ◆ Minneapolis

Learning to recognize and manage emotions is a huge part of growing up. Once you can think calmly and pause before you act, controlling emotions gets a whole lot easier. So come along with your furry, fabulous friends from *Sesame Street* as they teach you some easy ways to grow calmer, kinder, and more mindful.

Sincerely,

The editors at
Sesame Workshop

Table of Contents

Mindful Me

There's so much to do every day!

Being mindful and belly breathing can help you stay calm.

Elmo is having a hard time falling asleep!

But he knows what to do.
Elmo says good night to
each part of his body.

Now you try!

Start with your toes. Good night, toes. Good night, feet.
Good night, ankles. Good night, knees.

Telly is worried about the first day of music class.

Telly breathes. He focuses all of his attention on a fun triangle.

You try!

Look at something you really like.
Breathe slowly and focus on that one thing.

13

Cookie Monster
spills his milk.
**He feels so
embarrassed!**

But it's okay. He says something nice to himself.

Me smart cookie!

15

Now you try positive self-talk.

Everybody makes mistakes sometimes.
Remind yourself of some things you're
good at.

What can me say
to feel better?
Then me try
this again.

Rosita is sad! She has to leave her grandmother's house.

She shuts her eyes. Then she imagines a hug.

Can you try?

Just shut your eyes.
Then think of a hug.
You could even hug
a pillow. Feel better?

Everyone gets sad. But mindfulness helps us feel better.

Oh no! Abby broke her wand.

She's frustrated.

So she shuts her eyes. She does belly breathing and imagines blowing bubbles.

Can you blow bubbles too?

Breathe in slowly through your nose. Blow out through your mouth. Imagine blowing bubbles. Or try blowing real ones!

Sometimes Ernie feels lonely.

Then he thinks of Bert.
Ernie is thankful to
have a good friend.
He feels better.

You can be thankful. Think of people you are thankful for. Show them your love.

Being a mindful monster is easy.
And mindful monsters are happy monsters.

Stop and Smell the Flowers

Take a walk in your neighborhood. Pay attention to what is around you. Your mind stays quiet. You can be happy just to be where you are!

I love to smell the flowers at my park.

I prefer to smell stinky things.

Glossary

belly breathing: breathing slowly in through your nose and out through your mouth

focuses: thinks about one thing

imagines: makes a picture in the mind

mindful: a state of being where you slow down, pay attention, and relax

self-talk: saying things to yourself

Learn More

Ballard, Bronwen. *Your Mind Is like the Sky: A First Book of Mindfulness.* London: Frances Lincoln Children's Books, 2019.

Gates, Mariam. *Meditate with Me: A Step-by-Step Mindfulness Journey.* New York: Dial Books for Young Readers, 2017.

Verde, Susan. *I Am Peace: A Book of Mindfulness.* New York: Abrams Appleseed, 2019.

Try more mindfulness with *Sesame Street*. Have a parent or guardian download the free Breathe, Think, Do with Sesame app.

Index

Photo Acknowledgments

Image credits: Biletskiy_Evgeniy/iStock/Getty Images, pp. 4–5; DONOT6/iStock/Getty Images, p. 6; JGI/Tom Grill/Getty Images, p. 8; Westend61/Getty Images, p. 10; jovan_epn/iStock/Getty Images, p. 12; hartcreations/E+/Getty Images, p. 13; Fuse/Corbis/Getty Images, p. 14; serts/E+/Getty Images, p. 16; peterspiro/iStock/Getty Images, p. 18; PhotoAlto/Laurence Mouton/Getty Images, p. 20; SerrNovik/iStock/Getty Images, p. 21; 1933bkk/Shutterstock.com, p. 23; onebluelight/E+/Getty Images, p. 24; darrya/iStock/Getty Images, p. 25; monkeybusinessimages/iStock/Getty Images, p. 28. Design element: natrot/iStock/Getty Images (background waves).

Lerner Publications Company
An imprint of Lerner Publishing Group, Inc.
241 First Avenue North
Minneapolis, MN 55401 USA

For reading levels and more information, look up this title at www.lernerbooks.com.

Main body text set in Mikado.
Typeface provided by HVD fonts.

Editor: Allison Juda **Designer:** Lindsey Owens
Lerner team: Martha Kranes

Library of Congress Cataloging-in-Publication Data

Names: Kenney, Karen Latchana, author. | Children's Television Workshop. | Sesame street.
Title: Calm monsters, kind monsters : a Sesame Street guide to mindfulness / Karen Latchana Kenney.
Description: Minneapolis : Lerner Publications, 2020. | Includes index. | Audience: Ages 4–8 | Audience: Grades K–1 | Summary: "Breathing, thinking ahead, and calming down—mindfulness includes all this and more. Sesame Street characters present big emotions readers have likely faced alongside simple solutions like belly breathing to help kids cope with what they're feeling."– Provided by publisher.
Identifiers: LCCN 2019041630 (print) | LCCN 2019041631 (ebook) | ISBN 9781541590007 (library binding) | ISBN 9781728400617 (ebook)
Subjects: LCSH: Emotions—Juvenile literature.
Classification: LCC BF511 .K46 2020 (print) | LCC BF511 (ebook) | DDC 152.4—dc23

LC record available at https://lccn.loc.gov/2019041630
LC ebook record available at https://lccn.loc.gov/2019041631

Manufactured in the United States of America
1-47510-48054-1/28/2020

THE DIVERSITY OF LIFE

FROM SINGLE CELLS TO MULTICELLULAR ORGANIZATIONS

Robert Snedden

Series Editor
Andrew Solway

Heinemann Library
Chicago, Illinois

al Publishing

fessional Publishing,

nnlibrary.com

Designed by Paul Davies and Associates
Illustrations by Wooden Ark
Originated by Ambassador Litho Ltd.
Printed by Wing King Tong in Hong Kong

07 06 05 04
10 9 8 7 6 5 4 3 2

Library of Congress Cataloging-in-Publication Data
Snedden, Robert.
  The diversity of life : from single cells to multicellular organisms /
Robert Snedden.
        v. cm. -- (Cells & life)
Includes index.
Contents: A dazzling diversity -- What's in a name? -- Living kingdoms
-- All together now -- Mutations -- Genetic drift -- Natural selection
-- Adaptation -- Ripples in the gene pool -- Speciation -- Simple
beginnings -- A tour of the kingdoms -- Protistans -- Fungi -- Plants --
Plant evolution -- Animals -- A brief history of life -- The end of the
line -- The threat to diversity.
  ISBN 1-58810-673-X (HC), 1-58810-935-6 (Pbk.)
  1. Biological diversity--Juvenile literature. [1. Biological
diversity.] I. Title. II. Series.
  QH541.15.B56 S64 2002
  570--dc21
                        2001008582

Acknowledgments
The author and publishers are grateful to the following for permission to reproduce copyright material:
p.4 D.B. Fleetham/Oxford Scientific Films; p. 5 Digital Vision; p. 6a D. Fleetham/Oxford Scientific Films; p. 6b T. Bernhard/Oxford Scientific Films; p. 7 F. Schneidermeyer/Oxford Scientific Films; p. 9 K. Lounatmaa/Science Photo Library; p. 11 M. Tibbles/Oxford Scientific Films; p. 12/Garden Matters; p. 13 B. Kenmey/Oxford Scientific Films; p. 15 Science Photo Library; p. 16 K. Willson/Corbis; pp. 17, 26, 28 J. Burgess/Science Photo Library; p. 18 N. Rosing/Oxford Scientific Films; p. 19 L. Bush/Link; p. 20 J.B. Blossom/Survival Anglia; p. 21 S. North/Garden Matters; p. 22 G. Murti/Science Photo Library; p. 23 D. Phillips/Science Photo Library; p. 24 G. Ochoki/Science Photo Library; p. 25 A. and H-F Michler/Science Photo Library; p. 27 J. Howard/Science Photo Library; p. 29 I. West/Oxford Scientific Films; p. 30 J.C. Revy/Science Photo Library; p. 31 J. Watts/Science Photo Library; p. 32 B. Watts/Science Photo Library; p. 33 P. Goetgheluck/ Science Photo Library; p. 35 S. Meyers/Oxford Scientific Films; p. 36 Photo disc; p. 37 B. Goodale/Oxford Scientific Films; p. 39 David Dilcher and Ge Sun, University of Florida; p. 40 S. Stammers/Science Photo Library; p. 41 C. Palek/Oxford Scientific Films; p.42 G. Bernard/Science Photo Library; p. 43 Garden & Wildlife Matters;

Cover photograph reproduced with permission of Science Photo Library/Andrew Syred.

Our thanks to Richard Fosbery for his comments in the preparation of this book, and also to Alexandra Clayton.

Every effort has been made to contact copyright holders of any material reproduced in this book.
Any omissions will be rectified in subsequent printings if notice is given to the publisher.

Some words are shown in bold, **like this.** You can find out what they mean by looking in the glossary.